Encouraging Physical Activity in Infants

Moving Matters Series

Steve Sanders, EdD

Gryphon House
www.gryphonhouse.com

Copyright

Published by Gryphon House, Inc.
P. O. Box 10, Lewisville, NC 27023
800.638.0928; 877.638.7576 (fax)
Visit us on the web at www.gryphonhouse.com.

Bulk Purchase

Gryphon House books are available for special premiums and sales promotions as well as for fund-raising use. Special editions or book excerpts also can be created to specifications. For details, call 800.638.0928.

Disclaimer

Gryphon House, Inc., cannot be held responsible for damage, mishap, or injury incurred during the use of or because of activities in this book. Appropriate and reasonable caution and adult supervision of children involved in activities and corresponding to the age and capability of each child involved are recommended at all times. Do not leave children unattended at any time. Observe safety and caution at all times.

Library of Congress Cataloging-in-Publication Data

The Cataloging-in-Publication Data is registered with the Library of Congress for ISBN: 978-0-87659-245-8.

Contents

The Importance of
Physical Activity for Infants

You are wise to explore the physical development needs of the infant in your care. Naturally, babies need physical activity too— a child is never too young to move and learn about her body's capabilities. A newborn will undergo the greatest rate of physical development during her first year of life, and being physically active every day is important for her healthy growth and development. The physical skills that an infant acquires and masters now will serve as a foundation for skills such as running, jumping, throwing, catching, and striking that she will develop as a toddler and as a preschooler. Cultivating a base of physical skills gives children the tools to help them become physically active and healthy throughout life.

As in other areas of life, children rely on their caregivers and parents as role models and teachers when it comes to physical development. As you take on this role, this book will provide ideas for helping infants form a strong foundation for future physical activity. The activities presented are simple and straightforward—you will not need a lot of equipment—and they are also fun! You and the baby in your care will have a great time.

Please take note, however, that this book is not about making children into miniature athletes. If you help children develop some physical skills that someday help them participate in sports, then that is a bonus. Note that some parents want to push their children to become the best at throwing, catching, or kicking. Beware of this tendency because pushing children to achieve physical skills they are not ready for is developmentally inappropriate and may even be harmful.

During the first five years of life, movement plays an important part in all of a child's learning. Simply put, children learn about the world around them through movement, so those who are more efficient at moving are better able to explore and learn about their environment. Playing with and being physically active with an infant every day will help her develop critical movement skills. Experts agree that a baby whose muscles and senses are stimulated will become more receptive to her surroundings, leading to a fuller intellectual, emotional, and physical life.

For the purposes of this book, we define an infant as a child from birth to the age when she is able to walk. The skill of walking is a developmental

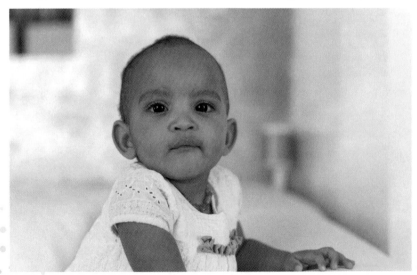

milestone that almost all children attain; however, all children do not walk at the same time. Most children will walk independently sometime between twelve and eighteen months of age. When a child stands up and begins taking her first steps, she becomes a toddler. Caregivers and parents then need a new set of guidelines and different kinds of activities to help promote the development of physical skills.

Guidelines for Infant Physical Activity

Guidelines for infant physical activity suggest that babies should be physically active several times daily, particularly through floor-based or tummy-time activities. The National Association for Sport and Physical Education (NASPE) has developed the *Active Start Physical Activity Guidelines for Children from Birth to Age 5*. NASPE advises that infants should have the following to promote healthy activity and movement:

- Daily interactions with parents or caregivers in physical activities that encourage them to move and explore the areas around them
- A care environment that promotes movement and active play for short periods several times daily
- Movement activities that encourage the infants to develop their physical skills
- The ability to move around in settings that at least meet, and ideally exceed, recommended safety standards for activities that exercise the body's large muscles
- Caregivers who understand the benefits of physical activity and foster the development of movement skills during structured and unstructured play

For further information, NASPE is now known as Shape America, and the guidelines are available via the website www.shapeamerica.org. You can find information on safety guidance for infant programs on the National Association for the Education of Young Children (NAEYC) website at http://families.naeyc.org.

What if a baby has a physical disability? Certainly, parents should check with the infant's doctor for advice. But keep in mind that children with disabilities will go through the same developmental progression as children without disabilities. If it is possible for a child with special needs to develop the same physical skills as other children, then that should be your goal. However, you may need to approach the activities in different ways to adapt to the child's abilities. Select the movements that are appropriate, and encourage development in those areas. The activities discussed in this book show caregivers and parents how to make play time and physical activity a constructive experience for all infants.

Learning How to Move

You may think an infant is too small or too young for physical activity; however, babies are naturally very active and should begin physical activity with parents and caregivers by six weeks of age. Physical activity for infants is all about learning how to move, and this is how they begin to learn about their world.

Your primary focus during these activities should be on establishing babies' motor skills, specifically balance and the promotion of muscle strength. Motor-skill development begins at birth with involuntary reflexes that take over the body and ensure that the baby starts to move. These reflexes go away as an infant gains voluntary control over his body. Without daily physical stimulation and movement, infants adopt more sedentary behaviors and tend to roll over, crawl, and walk later than babies who enjoy daily physical activity with a caregiver or parent.

Before an infant learns to crawl, physical activity will include reaching for and grasping objects, pulling and pushing, and moving the head and other body parts. Early physical exertion will also include stimulation of reflex movements by adults along with supervised routines and physical activities to promote balance and development of strength.

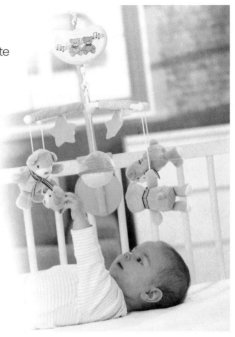

According to research discussed by educators Carl Gabbard and Luis Rodrigues in *Early Childhood News,* physical activity supports children's brain development and ability to become successful learners. Children use their bodies to explore their world. NASPE suggests that early motor skills serve as building blocks for future motor skillfulness; therefore, skill-building activities are important for children birth to age five.

As a baby nears his first birthday, he is likely to begin crawling. Several months later, he will begin walking. The activity sections of this book provide a number of specific ways to help infants strengthen their muscles and develop balance in anticipation of crawling and walking. Movement activities at this age should encourage children to explore and experiment with how their bodies move.

Research and experience have shown that active babies are more likely to sleep better at night, grow strong bones and muscles, and reach and maintain a healthy weight, as noted on the Active for Life (activeforlife.com) and KidsHealth (kidshealth.org) websites.. In addition, physically active infants are more likely to have an active lifestyle when they are older.

Supervise the infant at all times when working on gross motor skills, and make sure he has a safe space to practice movements. As the child grows, continue to revisit activities he enjoyed when he was younger, especially tummy-time activities. Introduce the child to new activities for developing gross motor skills when you feel he is ready. Remember, not all children progress at the same pace. Parents should talk to a pediatrician about any concerns about the child's motor development.

Infant Motor-Skill Milestones

The first year of a baby's life will be fast paced; you will be busy and active. Change happens daily. By the end of the first year, infants tend to almost triple their birth weight and grow 10 to 12 inches. During this time, most babies will advance from depending on reflexes for movement to being able to voluntarily move as they learn to roll over, crawl, sit up, stand, and maybe even walk. Exploring a new world and developing the physical skills to do so will consume the majority of the baby's time.

WHAT IS A DEVELOPMENTAL MILESTONE?

A *developmental milestone* is a skill infants acquire within a specific time frame—for example, sitting up without support. Most children learn the skill between the ages of five and seven months. Another developmental milestone for infants is walking, which typically occurs at about twelve to eighteen months of age.

Encouraging Physical Activity in Infants

Motor development can be divided into a discussion about gross motor skills and fine motor skills. Babies develop fine motor skills to control the movement of the small muscles of the body, specifically their hands and fingers. Fine motor skills include such actions as holding a spoon, grasping small objects, turning pages in a book, or even using the lips and tongue to taste food. The infant's developing vision directly relates to learning fine motor skills, which we will discuss in more detail in the section on tracking and vision skills.

Gross motor skills are the movements infants learn to control the large muscles of the body, including moving the arms, legs, and feet. These skills provide infants with opportunities to move and interact with their environment. They will learn to sit without support and pull up to a standing position while holding onto furniture. As children get older, they will learn more advanced gross motor skills: walking, running, climbing, jumping, rolling, kicking, throwing, catching, and striking. Most gross motor skills are acquired during childhood over a relatively short period of time between birth and about age twelve. However, most experts agree that the foundation of gross motor skills in children typically is learned by about age six, and after that time children are working to become more efficient with the motor-skill patterns they have developed.

The first year of life lays the foundation for further development of gross motor skills as a toddler and preschooler. Having a good basis of these skills will eventually help children participate in the sports and recreational activities needed to be physically active and healthy as they grow. Motor skills don't just develop on their own. Infants must learn to engage in motor activities in combination with their physical growth.

As you plan activities and incorporate them into the infant's daily routine, keep them fun and appropriate. If the baby shows frustration, stop and come back to the activity at a later time. Because you are the infant's role model and teacher, make sure you play with her and are physically active together every day.

NOT WALKING, BUT MOVING— DID YOU KNOW?

Infants who are not yet walking need exercise, too! The physical activity that caregivers and parents do with infants who are not yet walking can help with the following:

- Maintaining a healthy weight
- Developing good posture, strength, balance, and tracking skills
- Keeping their bodies active and learning about their new environment
- Developing their senses of hearing, sight, and touch

Strengthening Muscles for Coordination

Growth and development start from the head and move downward, and from the center of the body and move outward. At birth, a child's head is about 70 percent of its adult size. To gain control of her head, the infant will first need to strengthen her neck and shoulder muscles. As that process moves forward, she will also begin moving to strengthen muscles in the trunk, then the legs, the feet, and the hands. By the end of the first year, most infants will have developed the muscle control and strength to begin walking.

During the first year of life, muscles and bones grow quickly, and children who are active can increase their coordination and strength. At birth, physical movements will appear random and without purpose. By the time an infant is six months of age, however, movement will become more purposeful and focused.

Infants develop their motor skills in a specific and predictable sequential order. But the rate at which a particular infant reaches developmental milestones likely will be different from other infants the same age. No two babies go through these physical milestones at exactly the same time. Infants may also spend different amounts of time at each stage before moving on to the next stage.

Developmental charts can help you see the averages for when infants tend to reach motor milestones. Remember, however, that the figures are only averages, and a specific infant's achievement of the milestones

HEAD SIZE— DID YOU KNOW?

At birth, a child's head is about one-third the size of her entire body. By age two, the proportion changes, and the head is about one-quarter the size of the body. By adulthood, the head is about one-eighth the size of the body.

might vary by several months in either direction, depending on genetics and on the child's daily movement experiences. Experts note that the environment plays a major role in infant physical development. What parents and caregivers do to enrich the infant's play environment often can affect the time it takes for the child to reach developmental milestones. However, adults should not push their infants to perform skills before they are developmentally ready. This type of pressure can lead the infant to become frustrated. Babies should be allowed to acquire motor skills at their own pace. Parents and caregivers need to provide physical activity and play opportunities for infants every day in a fun, stress-free environment. This helps form the strength and balance needed to develop physical skills.

Encouraging Physical Activity in Infants

Developmental Progression

What is the progression of learning an infant will go through in reaching developmental milestones? The following list outlines the developmental motor highlights of the first year and the average time it takes for an infant to reach these milestones:

- Two months—is able to lift head up while lying on stomach
- Three months—can roll over
- Four months—can sit propped up without falling over
- Six months—is able to sit up without support
- Seven months—begins to stand while holding on to things for support
- Nine months—can begin to walk using support
- Ten months—is able to momentarily stand without support
- Twelve months—begins walking alone without support

To reach these milestones, babies need to start moving. Get ready! It is time for the infant's first exercise class.

Creating
the Best
Environment for
Physical
Activity

Infants should be engaged in physical activity anytime they are awake and interested. Inspire the infant from the beginning by providing an environment that includes a variety of appropriate equipment and the space needed to move. Plan activities that help the infant reach developmental milestones, such as sitting, crawling, and walking. Such activities are described in later chapters of this book.

Some of the most important ingredients in the physical-activity environment are involved caregivers and parents who schedule time each day to play and be physically active with the infant. During the baby's first year, he will be bonding with and learning to trust caregivers. This trust includes or is based on an understanding that adults are there to help. This trust

will help him feel secure when you do movement activities together that introduce him to the world of motor development and physical activity.

Providing a Secure Space

You have the responsibility for providing both structured and unstructured physical activity and play time for the infant, and you should build frequent activity into the baby's routine. Infants will benefit from a combination of indoor and outdoor play time.

Space is essential to movement, and babies need a predictable space in which to move and learn. A predictable home environment suggests that the area is safe, that adults are present supervising and playing with the infant, that there is plenty of room to move, and that there are routines that guide learning about physical activity. The environment should also be organized and equipped with lots of age-appropriate play materials and toys. Remember, when the infant was born, she had no knowledge of what her new world would be like. Make the infant's world interesting, exciting, and fun, but also provide for a predictable space and routine so the baby feels secure.

During the first year of life, an infant will be involved with locomotion, the ability to move from one place to another. Soon the entire home or child care environment will be at the disposal of the curious infant—and you will need to plan accordingly. For healthy development, physical activity should be part of the daily routine. Infants respond well to short periods of play and movement, and a good goal is at least two to three times each day. You might start with three-minute periods and build up to thirty minutes as the baby gets older. Even though physical activity for young children primarily occurs through unstructured, active play, adult supervision is always required.

- Physical activity during the first six months takes place in the form of tummy time and includes reaching for and grasping objects, strengthening back and neck muscles, moving and stretching arms and legs, improving balance, and learning how to roll over.

- During the second six months, physical activity is expanded as the infant moves to further increase her strength and balance to learn the basic movement skills of crawling, standing, and walking.

- Infants have an internal need to move and be physically active. This is how they learn about their world. Provide time and space for infants to explore and practice physical skills.

- Make sure the environment has enough open space and age-appropriate toys and equipment, including some that infants can use for support to help pull themselves up and balance.

Letting Infants Explore

Parents and caregivers can help by encouraging infants to explore—everything from their toes and hands to toys and rattles. Babies also benefit from exploring and interacting with people. Exploration time can begin at about six weeks of age and should take place on the floor every day. You can place the baby on a colorful quilt or activity mat, but make sure blankets are baby safe to avoid danger of suffocation. Do not let the baby sleep on his tummy, as he could suffocate at this young age. Set aside some time for the infant to explore on his own and also have time where you sit and explore together. Place him on his back or side, and place a variety of colorful objects with different textures around him. Observe as he reaches out to grasp items, holds them in his hands, and shakes them.

Infants explore their world with their hands and with their mouths. They do not know what is safe and what is unsafe to put in their mouths, so make sure toys are clean and frequently washed. Make sure the objects and toys will not fit into his mouth so you eliminate choking hazards. Keep medicines, household cleaners, and cosmetics away from the play area. Supervision is an important key to avoiding accidents while a child explores his environment. Unlike adults, infants have not experienced danger; therefore, adults must be the eyes and ears of infants to keep them protected.

Creating Activity Routines

Being on a schedule is comforting to infants. Babies need routines as much as adults do. Infants like to know that certain things will happen at a regular time each day. Infants will begin to recognize patterns in their days at about three to four months—for example, by four months most babies know the difference between night and day.

You can begin creating a daily physical-activity routine with an infant between about six weeks and three months, but this is not the time to place her on a strict schedule. Gradually add a physical-activity routine to an infant's daily schedule over a period of several weeks. Routines do not develop overnight, and adult consistency is the key to success. As an infant becomes a toddler and then a preschooler, she will recognize the importance of having time for physical activity in her daily routine.

Over time, infants naturally will develop certain routines, such as when to sleep and eat. In addition to planned activity times, physical-activity routines can happen any time throughout the day. For example, you might start each morning with infant leg and arm stretches or do a few strength and balance activities right after diaper changes.

It takes time for a baby to develop a predictable routine, and it will happen when you present daily activities in a predictable sequence. For example, plan midmorning and afternoon activity times. During these times, participate in physical activities in the same order and repeat the sequence daily to help the infant expect the familiar activities. Routines should be simple and not strict—you do not need an activity routine that is timed down to the minute. Be flexible! This can be a fun time as an infant develops new skills and explores her world.

The time of day you have physical activity is important. Certainly do not plan these activities before or after eating or right after an infant wakes up from a nap. Experiment with different times to see what works best for both of you. As the baby grows, particularly between four and twelve months, awake time will become longer. As this happens, you can increase the amount of time each day devoted to physical activity. Don't

A stimulating home physical-activity environment for infants includes the following elements:

- Appropriate space for movement
- Daily tummy time to improve strength and balance
- Daily routine and a plan for physical activity every day
- Repetition of physical activities to learn motor skills
- A variety of appropriate equipment and toys

force a routine on an infant if she is not yet ready to willingly follow it. If a baby appears upset with a part of the activity routine, stop and revisit the activity another day. When you try again, perhaps the infant will be more comfortable with the movement.

Here are some ideas for establishing physical-activity routines.

- After about six weeks, make sure to put tummy time or floor play in her routine at least one time daily. Start with three to five minutes and extend up to twenty to thirty minutes. Start the tummy-time routine by laying the infant on her stomach. Your job is to sit beside the infant and relax and observe as she explores using her hands and feet, and spends time looking around at her environment. You can talk and sing to the baby also.

- Over time, add rattles and soft toys to the tummy-time routine, and then get involved helping the infant stretch and learn to balance.
- Pay attention to the infant's needs. Let her take the lead. Don't force physical activity on her when she is tired or hungry.
- Take the baby for a daily walk in the stroller. For parents, especially, this is a good time to get out of the house and fit in a walk for themselves.
- Play cheerful, upbeat music during play time. The baby will soon recognize that music is related to fun physical activity.
- Build your routine. Lay a quilt or mat on the floor, and place the infant in the middle of it. Participate with her in some of the stretching activities found in Chapter 6. Start with one or two activities, and add a couple more to the routine each week. Do these activities in the same order each day for short periods of time. Eventually add rattles and soft toys.
- Make sure there is free play time in an infant's routine. Lay out the blanket and toys and let her explore.
- Don't force the physical-activity routine—lots of things can get in the way. Travel can disrupt the schedule; or if the child is sick or teething, you may need to start over with the routine when she is well again.
- Understand that routines will change as the infant grows.

Encouraging Physical Activity in Infants

Joining Playgroups

Many parents ask, "Should I join a playgroup with my infant?" Certainly a physical-activity playgroup is beneficial for toddlers and preschoolers. At that age, children benefit from the social interaction of playing with other children their age and from watching others participate in physical activities. Group play can give toddlers and preschoolers a chance to learn new motor skills as they play and socialize with other children.

The infant may enjoy the social interaction of having other babies around, but it is questionable whether this interaction will make a difference in his physical development before he is walking. At this stage, it may be more important for parents and caregivers to establish a daily physical-activity routine and bond with the infant than to add additional distractions.

Playgroups do provide opportunities for adults to talk with other adults about infant development and to share ideas. Going to a playgroup one or two times each week is a good outlet for parents who may be at home alone all day long. It gives them an activity outside the home that allows them to make friends and enjoy adult conversation and support.

If you decide to participate in an infant playgroup, find one that works with the baby's daily routine. A group that meets at an out-of-the-way location or during the infant's nap time or mealtime probably will not be the right fit. When you do join a group, look for one that includes no more

than four adults and the children in their care. Limiting the group size will help keep the infant from being overstimulated and fussy during play time. Activities during playgroup should be similar to those you do at home so you maintain consistency with the established routine.

Again, there is no hurry to join a group, but having a physical-activity playgroup will give infants in home-based care opportunities to socialize and watch other babies and adults interact. Even babies who are not yet ready to roll over or crawl will enjoy watching people and will be entertained.

Age-Appropriate Equipment

Toys, equipment, and other physical-activity materials for infants should give them opportunities to practice and use their gross motor skills. If equipment is needed for individual activities listed in this book, that is noted with the activity description. Most activities for helping develop strength and balance really do not require a lot of equipment.

Materials for infant physical activity include items such as blankets, rattles, mobiles, blocks, a plastic beach ball, and other small balls (but not small enough to be a choking hazard). A large cardboard box could be used as a tunnel when an infant begins crawling. Toys that make music or noises are great entertainment, and playing music during physical-activity time can signal that it is time for activity and fun. Play objects should be of different sizes, colors, shapes, weights, and textures. Furniture that is in the play area should be solid and stable, as the infant will soon be pulling herself up to stand while holding on to available furniture. Parents and caregivers should regularly check equipment to make sure all available materials remain safe for the infant to use.

Infants need room to stretch and move; they should not spend more than twenty minutes each day strapped into equipment that confines their movement when they are awake. Doctors do not recommend using equipment such as walkers, infant jumpers, and baby swings. Some adults think these items will help an infant walk at an early age; however, research from the American Academy of Pediatrics (AAP) suggests that infants who are put in baby jumpers or walkers do not walk any sooner than other children. Also, the AAP strongly advises against using walkers because babies can get injured when moving around in them. Furthermore, crawling, standing, and walking skills may be delayed when walkers are used, and an infant may fall behind in other areas of development because such equipment restricts the ability to move and explore.

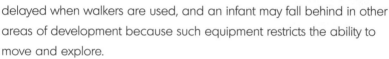

Promoting Safety

Infant safety is the first priority in the physical-activity environment. It really is hard for adults to see everything in the environment that could be a safety concern. A great way to understand the hazards of the environment is to get down on the floor, on your hands and knees, and look at things as if you were an infant. Parents and caregivers may be surprised at what they find when they look at the world from a child's perspective. One thing is constant—the more physical skills a baby learns, the more trouble he can get into.

Here are some ideas of things to look for when you are on your hands and knees on the floor examining the environment from a child's point of view.

- Are electrical cords and cords to blinds placed out of reach?
- Do all electrical outlets have outlet covers?
- Are toys lightweight, large enough not to be swallowed, and without sharp points or edges?

- Is furniture secured or heavy enough not to topple over if an infant decides to climb?
- Is there a safe blanket or mat for the infant to play on?
- Are the carpet and hard floor clean? A baby is going to put everything he can find in his mouth. Yes, everything.
- Have you removed any cleaning chemicals and placed them at a high level away from the baby?
- Have you made sure all toys are kept clean? Wash toys at least weekly.

Don't forget the infant's crib: Safety standards require that crib bars be no more than $2^3/_8$ inches apart so that a child cannot get his head or body parts stuck. The mattress should be snug in the frame. Fluffy pillows, stuffed animals, or large comforters are not recommended in an infant's crib during the first year.

You do not need a long list of things to do to make the infant's physical-activity environment safe. Most caregivers and parents childproof the environment naturally. Each time you enter a new space, you will instinctively begin to look around and note the things you need to move or at least be aware of to keep the baby safe. The best direction is to clear out a room and simply have a large empty space devoted to the

Encouraging Physical Activity in Infants

- Supervise the baby closely at all times, but do not restrain his movements.
- Toys should not have sharp edges or pieces that can be swallowed.
- Provide lightweight, brightly colored toys with a variety of textures.
- Lay out a 5'x 7' blanket or quilt for the infant to roll and play on.
- Infant play should always be at ground level. Tables or counters are not appropriate places for safe physical activity.
- Consider taking a course in infant CPR to understand how to deal with a choking baby.

baby, but this is not always practical. Even with a cleared-out space, parents and caregivers need to supervise babies to keep them safe.

Parents and caregivers will naturally have concerns about safety—but don't overlook the simple things you can do to keep the baby safe. There is no foolproof way to protect an infant at all times. You must continuously work to make sure the physical-activity environment is safe and must watch the baby at all times. Infants are simply too young to know how to stay safe on their own.

Reflexes:
Moving for
Survival

CHAPTER

3

Reflexes are very important in the process of a child's physical-skill development. The infant was born with reflexes to aid in survival and to help stimulate the development of the physical skills that she will need to roll over, crawl, and, eventually, walk.

During the first several weeks and months of a baby's life, you will notice her twitching, stretching, jerking, and kicking at different times during the day. Do not be alarmed; all these involuntary movements are a sign to parents that everything is working as nature planned. Because a newborn cannot survive on her own, her body has prewired abilities called *reflexes*. When they are born, babies are equipped with primitive reflexes to help them begin moving and learning about their new world. These particular reflexes are normal in infants but not in other age groups.

Reflexes are automatic reactions to stimulation that enable infants to respond to the environment before any learning has taken place. For example, babies automatically suck when presented  with a nipple, turn their heads when an adult speaks, grasp at a finger that is pressed into their hand, and startle when exposed to loud noises. Some reflexes, such as blinking, are permanent. Others, such as grasping, disappear after several months and eventually become voluntary responses, suggesting that the baby's brain sends out a message to her muscles to grasp an object.

Understanding the importance of these reflexes and providing activities that stimulate them will help adults give babies a good start in the development of physical skills. Reflexes also help identify normal brain and nerve activity. Much of a baby's activity and movement in her first weeks of life is based on reflexes. For example, when you put your finger in her mouth, she doesn't think about what to do but instead sucks automatically. When she sees a bright light, she will tightly shut her eyes, because that is what her reflexes make her do. When you hold a child upright and then quickly place her body forward as if she's falling, she will extend her arms forward as if to break a fall.

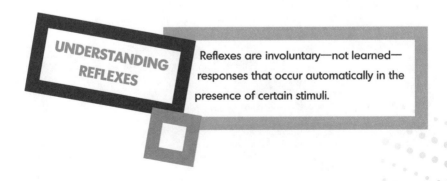

UNDERSTANDING REFLEXES

Reflexes are involuntary—not learned—responses that occur automatically in the presence of certain stimuli.

Reflexes are automatic movements that are directed from a child's brain stem, but they involve no thought—the action just happens spontaneously in response to certain stimulation—and some occur only in specific periods of development. Certain sensations or movements around the child produce specific muscle responses. As a child's brain matures and takes control of body movement, she no longer needs the reflexes, and they disappear. Then the child's brain and muscles take over to work together in moving the body.

The physical development of an infant begins with these involuntary reflexes working to move the body in order to survive. Reflexes help a child to initially feed herself by nursing and then to gain control of her body to move in and control the physical environment. Even though all infants initially use these reflexes to gain control of their bodies and then to acquire physical skills, the rate at which motor skills are developed varies from child to child.

STIMULATING REFLEXES— DID YOU KNOW?

The presence and strength of a reflex is an important sign of nervous-system development and function. Infant reflexes are not needed in later childhood and adulthood, and their persistence may hinder the child's brain development and can be a major contributor to physical and other developmental problems. By stimulating infant reflexes, parents and caregivers will help prevent delays in physical (motor) development. Immediately after birth and throughout the first year, the pediatrician will check the infant's reflexes during well-baby checkups.

Encouraging Physical Activity in Infants

To illustrate the importance of infant reflexes during the first weeks and months of a baby's life and how those reflexes lead her to grow and develop physically, let's look at the rectal reflex. One of the most important reflexes all children have, the rectal reflex helps a baby have bowel movements. The rectum is the part of the infant's bowel that is closest to the anus. When the rectum fills, this triggers the rectal reflex, which helps to push out the contents so the baby can have a bowel movement. An infant has no control over this process and relies on the reflex. For most children, the brain and muscles begin working together to control this reflex sometime between the ages of two and four. Adults may notice that babies appear to strain and sometimes get red in the face during bowel movements. They are not constipated—this action is just a normal part of the rectal reflex working.

Activities to Stimulate Infant Reflexes

So you may wonder what the important infant reflexes are and how you can stimulate them to promote physical activity in a child. Without adequate physical stimulation, infants adopt more sedentary behaviors and tend to roll over, crawl, and walk later than babies who enjoy daily physical activity with an adult.

Giving an infant space and freedom of movement will encourage him to explore his environment and learn about his body. Playpens, swings, and infant seats may be appropriate at certain times, but allow the infant time to move around freely with close supervision. You should try to stimulate infant reflexes, but don't be alarmed if the baby doesn't always cooperate. You may not be performing the stimulus perfectly, or the baby might be too tired or hungry to respond.

Rooting Reflex

One of the first reflexes you will notice in a newborn infant is the *rooting reflex,* which helps a baby find food. You can stimulate the rooting reflex

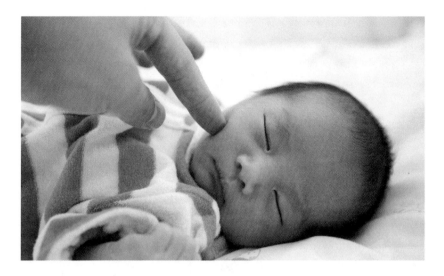

by touching or stroking a baby's cheek along the side of his mouth. The infant will turn his head and open his mouth as he tries to find something to suck. In some babies, this reflex may last as long as twelve months, but it usually disappears around four to five months. Parents and caregivers should not mistake the rooting reflex as a sign of hunger, as infants will turn their heads and open their mouths any time their cheeks are stroked, even if they are not hungry.

Sucking Reflex

The *sucking reflex* is automatic when a finger, nipple, or pacifier is inserted into the infant's mouth. Sucking helps the infant initially to find food, but it also helps him learn about his new world. The sucking reflex is instinctive and directs the child to suck on anything that gets close to his mouth. Adults should make sure that a newborn's environment is clear of any small items that could be a choking hazard; even buttons or jewelry that adults are wearing could be dangerous to an infant who is trying to find something to suck.

Most infants will want to suck even when they are not feeding, as the action has a calming effect on them. This tendency is normal and is one reason the use of a pacifier has become popular. The sucking reflex usually disappears around three to four months, and adults may find that this is a good time for the pacifier to disappear also.

Encouraging Physical Activity in Infants

Tongue-Thrust Reflex

The *tongue-thrust reflex* can help you know when the infant is ready to eat solid foods. The tongue thrust can be observed by touching the baby's lips or by touching a baby spoon to the tip of his tongue. The baby's tongue will automatically move forward, which aids him in feeding from a breast or bottle. This is an important reflex related to a child's early safety, as the reflex prevents him from choking on objects he may place in his mouth. When the reflex disappears, the child is ready to eat solid foods. But if parents introduce solid foods while the reflex is still active, the tongue will be in the way and the infant will push the food out. This reflex disappears around four to six months of age. If you attempt to feed a baby solid food at this age, and he continually pushes the food out of his mouth, this does not indicate a dislike for the food. It is a sign that the infant is simply not ready to eat solid foods.

Hand-to-Mouth Reflex

To get things into their mouths, infants have a *hand-to-mouth reflex* that complements the rooting and sucking reflexes. This reflex can be observed by stroking the infant's cheek or the palm of his hand. This stimulation causes the baby to root and his arm to flex and bring the hand to the mouth. When the hand gets to the baby's mouth, the sucking reflex takes over and the baby begins to learn he has hands and fingers. This reflex also helps the infant understand that movement of the hand and arm toward the middle of the body helps to gently rock the body sideways. Over time, this action will help a child develop the strength to roll over on his side. Parents and caregivers should not mistake sucking on hands or fingers as a sign of hunger. It is just another reflex action at work.

Tonic Neck Reflex

Place the infant on his back and make a sound with your voice or with a rattle from either side of the child's body. The baby's *tonic neck reflex* will take over. He will turn his head in the direction of the sound to hear and see, then his arm on that side will extend toward the sound, followed by the leg on the same side. The turning of the head also activates the vestibular (balance) system through the shifting of the fluid in the inner ears.

Adults can experience this reflex on their own: First, turn your head to one side and let your arm follow in the same direction. See how easy it is to move your arm when your head turns first? Now, try to

Encouraging Physical Activity in Infants

move your arm without turning your head. The movement does not flow and is more difficult. These reflex movements are helping to strengthen the child's muscles, getting him ready to turn his head and follow with his arm and then his leg to roll over several months from now.

You can help the infant begin to strengthen these muscles by stimulating the tonic neck reflex several times each day. Simply make a noise on one side of the body and watch the reflex at work. Make sure that you stimulate the reflex on both sides of the body. The tonic neck reflex usually disappears at five to seven months of age.

Startle Reflex

The *startle* or *Moro reflex* is present at birth and can last up to six months but normally disappears by three to four months of age. The reflex occurs when there is an unexpected or loud noise or when the baby's head suddenly shifts position. The reflex can also be seen when the temperature changes abruptly (such as when you change the infant's clothes).

When startled by an unexpected noise or loss of balance, the infant's legs and head extend and the arms jerk up and out. The infant's palms will first be open as the arms are extended, but as the arms come back toward the body, the hands will be clenched into fists as if trying to grasp onto something. To stimulate the reflex, carry the infant facing you and bend forward or to the side quickly. As the infant loses balance, the reflex causes him to extend his arms and grab onto you to keep from falling.

Remember that infant reflex movements do not happen by the infant's choice but are activated only when stimulated. As the infant grows and develops, movements that were once activated by stimulation become integrated into the higher functions of the brain. Movement will then be in the child's control.

Most infants cry loudly when the startle reflex is stimulated. The reflex is sometimes mistaken as a sign of fear, but it is really just a protective action to try to grasp something and avoid falling.

Grasp Reflex

The *grasp reflex* is another automatic response to stimulation that helps a child better understand his surroundings and begin the process of strengthening muscles and controlling the movement of his body. Infants have such strong grasps that they can almost be lifted up if both hands are grasping your fingers.

The grasp reflex only lasts two to three months, so it is important to stimulate it early and often. To stimulate this reflex, simply touch the palm of the infant's hand. He will grab your finger and hold on tight. Trying to remove the finger causes the grip to tighten. This reflex helps the baby hold onto people or objects, so make sure you stimulate both hands. Holding on tightly does not mean a baby is scared—it is just an automatic response to the stimulation. The grasp reflex also can be

observed by stimulating the bottom of the infant's feet. Although the baby cannot make a fist with his foot, if you stroke the bottom of one foot, the grasp reflex will work to curl up his toes.

Walking or Step Reflex

The *walking reflex* is present at birth and may prepare the baby developmentally for walking. Hold the infant upright with your hands under his armpits and his feet hanging, and then lower him so his feet touch the floor. The baby will lift one foot and then the other as if walking. It is interesting that this reflex disappears at about two months, and yet infants do not begin walking for several months after that. Although this reflex is short lived, this stepping action will appear again at about eight months or so when a child begins to voluntarily raise his feet and take steps. At that point, the infant enters the world of big body movement—then life changes for everyone.

Righting Reflex

Ever wonder how you learned to place your hand in front of you to break a fall? It all started with the *righting reflex*. Lay the infant on his back, and place a lightweight, see-through scarf over his face. He will automatically shake his head from side to side and wave his arms until the scarf is pushed away. This is the infant's way of protecting himself. The righting reflex can also be seen at other times. For example, sometime around four to six months, the infant will begin learning how to sit up on his own. Watch when he begins to fall over—he will stick his hand out in an attempt to catch himself. The reflex begins to disappear after twelve months when the infant begins to develop strength and control of his body.

Parachute Reflex

Similar to the righting reflex is the *parachute reflex*, which helps the baby catch himself if he begins to fall. This reflex appears in older infants at about five to six months but before the infant is able to walk. Hold the child upright facing away from you and rotate his body quickly forward as if he is falling. The infant will extend his arms forward as if to break a fall.

Some reflexes stay with the child throughout life. The following list provides examples of reflexes that last into adulthood:

- Blinking reflex—blinking the eyes when they are touched or when a sudden bright light appears
- Cough reflex—coughing when the airway is stimulated
- Gag reflex—gagging when the throat or back of the mouth is stimulated
- Sneeze reflex—sneezing when the nasal passages are irritated
- Yawn reflex—yawning when the body needs more oxygen

Swimming Reflex

Place the infant lying facedown on a blanket. When the swimming reflex hits, he will kick his legs and make a paddle motion with his arms, like he is attempting to swim. You would also be able to see the baby paddle and kick in a swimming motion if you placed him facedown in a pool of water; however, this is not advisable. Playing with the baby in a swimming pool can be fun, but allowing the infant to be submerged can be risky, as infants can swallow large amounts of water. Swim lessons and learning to swim can wait until the child has better muscular control of his body. The

American Academy of Pediatrics advises that children are not ready for formal swimming lessons until they are at least four years old, even though infant swim classes are popular with many parents. The swimming reflex disappears at about six months of age.

Strengthening Muscles and Making Connections

Several important reflexes are related to the infant's survival, including sucking, rooting, and the tongue thrust. Other reflexes, such as the grasping, swimming, stepping, and tonic neck reflexes, help form the basis for complex motor skills that will develop later in life. During the tonic neck reflex when the child's hand crosses in front of the body, she will naturally look at the hand in front of her eyes. This movement encourages the child to combine vision with arm movements and eventually reach for different objects around the body.

When the stepping reflex is exercised regularly, the infant will display more spontaneous stepping movements and will gain muscle strength. The grasping reflex prepares the infant to eventually be able to pick up a ball and throw it at a target.

Movement and physical activity are important to muscle and nerve growth. With babies, movement begins with infant reflexes, which help connect the muscles to the brain so physical activity and movement can take place.

CONCERNS ABOUT TIMING

You might wonder if you should be concerned if a child is slow to demonstrate reflexes or if the reflexes do not disappear when they should. The child's pediatrician will usually discover abnormal infant reflexes during well-baby visits. If you notice an infant's reflexes continuing after they should have disappeared, parents should discuss this with the child's doctor.

Promoting Activity to Nurture Development

When the infant is ready to advance beyond reflex movements, you can promote physical development by exploring the sense of touch and experimenting with tummy-time activities.

Textures, Shapes, and the Sense of Touch

The sense of touch is important to all young children who are learning how to move. Touching stimulates sensors within the muscles and joints that help the infant develop a sense of the orientation of his limbs and body in space, which is called *proprioception.* Learning any new motor skill involves the proprioceptive senses. Without proprioception, humans would, for example, need to consciously watch our feet to make sure that we stay upright while walking, or watch our hands when feeding ourselves or when attempting to throw a ball. As infants use touch to develop strength and increase their flexibility, they are improving their proprioceptive senses.

Being touched is part of the birth process and is an important element of a baby's first contact with the world. The sense of touch is part of the tactile system. The system includes the nerves under the surface of the baby's skin that send signals to the brain. When pressure or a light touch is applied to a baby's skin, nerves signal the brain. When the temperature changes, nerves signal the brain. This interaction between the nerves and the brain plays an important role in helping the infant understand his environment and react to changes in his surroundings. Newborn babies do not have the experience to differentiate among shapes, sizes, patterns, colors, and textures; touching helps them learn about the characteristics of objects in their environment. Every time an infant uses his sense of touch, he is creating a new memory that will help him learn other skills in the future.

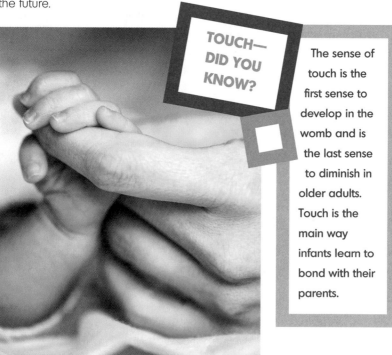

TOUCH— DID YOU KNOW?

The sense of touch is the first sense to develop in the womb and is the last sense to diminish in older adults. Touch is the main way infants learn to bond with their parents.

Encouraging Physical Activity in Infants

Through touch, babies learn a sense of trust while being held by parents and other caregivers. When you cuddle, kiss, and hug an infant, you are strengthening the bond between you. By reaching out and exploring, they learn spatial awareness and begin to understand that they can control parts of their environment by touching and holding onto people and objects. By investigating varied textures, babies come to understand similarities and differences in materials and purposes. As their explorations advance, they learn about cause and effect in terms of how a certain texture feels and whether or not it is safe to touch.

As babies strive to reach toys and other objects, they need to use their muscles and joints to stretch. As an infant manipulates an item, his hands and body will send signals to his brain to help him better recognize the textures, patterns, and shapes that make up his new environment.

You can stimulate the infant's investigations by providing a range of textures and temperatures, such as a cool metal spoon and a warm fuzzy blanket. Infants and toddlers will quickly learn that they can be more successful playing with a ball that has a textured surface that they can grip onto as opposed to a slippery surface.

As infants go through the process of learning about soft, rough, and hard surfaces and textures, they will certainly have some little accidents. These minor bumps (for example, bumping the nose on the side of the crib) actually teach infants about the importance of understanding the properties of different surfaces. As babies grow, they will identify for themselves the surfaces they should stay away from or be cautious around while active (the hard side of the crib) and the surfaces they can feel comfortable leaning against (a soft toy or a caregiver's shoulder). Still, caregivers need to make sure that such little bumps are not repeated often.

Giving the infant different textures to explore will encourage him to start reaching for and grasping objects and thus develop grip strength. Eventually, the child will be able to grip objects and throw them, pick up food and eat it, grasp and hold onto a ladder rung when climbing, and clutch and turn the handles to steer a tricycle. Exposure to objects of different shapes, sizes, and textures will also help when the child begins to develop fine motor skills such as stringing beads, zipping and buttoning clothing, and holding and writing with crayons and pencils.

Be sure that textured materials are safe. Watch out for sharp edges or items that may be too cold or too hot. Provide a variety of different textures for the infant to play with during tummy time.

- Use blankets in a variety of materials.
- Provide different types of fabrics to play with (flannel, satin, cotton, rough, silky, and smooth).
- Use a silky scarf to pull gently across the infant's hands and feet.
- Find a small plastic bottle with a secure cap and fill it with water. Chill it in the fridge, and then let the infant experience what a cool or cold object feels like.

- Provide a variety of small, textured rubber and plastic balls for the infant to grasp.

For older babies, try some of these investigations:

- Provide the infant with colorful toys that have smooth, bumpy, and irregular surfaces.
- Provide a safe zone when infants are experimenting with touch, and be sure only soft, safe toys and items are reachable in the zone.
- Encourage crawling on different surfaces (carpet, wood floor, or grass).

As infants begin to move into eating solid foods, they love to explore the different textures of the menu items. This activity will get messy, but the way babies understand the textures of food is through touch. Provide opportunities to explore soft foods such as mashed potatoes, cooked vegetables, and mashed bananas.

Tummy-Time Activities

Tummy time is not just about a baby lying on the floor on her tummy; it is more active than you might think. Activities should begin at six weeks of age, when the baby is beginning to stay awake for longer periods of time and is ready to explore. You will see, though, that preparation for tummy time begins much sooner.

There are many benefits to play time on the stomach, including learning the physical skills that are essential for later development. Babies lift their heads to investigate the world and in doing so begin to strengthen their neck and upper-back muscles. During tummy time, infants will strengthen muscles as they kick their feet and move their arms. These movements encourage overall muscle development and get infants ready to later roll over from the back to the tummy and from the tummy to the back.

Play Time, Practice Time

In later sections, we will discuss the importance of developing strength, balance, and tracking skills. But before moving on, let's explore some of the different kinds of activities that might be practiced during tummy time.

To start tummy time, place a quilt or mat on the floor, and lay the baby on his tummy. This is not a time for the parent or caregiver to have a break in the hectic day; it is a fun play time for both you and the child, but adult supervision is a must. Start tummy time gradually. The infant may only last ten to fifteen seconds during his first tummy-time session. Always stop the session if the infant appears upset with the activity. Come back and try tummy time later.

Tummy-time activities can also be done with the baby on your tummy as you lie on the floor or by laying the baby facedown across your lap. He

Encouraging Physical Activity in Infants

can then raise his head to look directly at you or across the room. Hold your hands firmly on the baby's back in case he begins to slip off.

The baby may initially resist tummy time because he does not have control of his head. But he will catch on soon, and head control is the first skill he will master. In addition to exercising the neck and back muscles, the raising of the head helps improve balance, so the infant can hold his head steady when he is being carried. Tummy time helps the child meet key physical milestones such as rolling over, sitting alone, crawling, and pulling up to stand.

There are no set guidelines for the amount of time the six-week-old should spend on his stomach each day. Start gradually with a few minutes at a time and work up to ten to fifteen minutes two or three times each day. By about three months of age, the baby should get at least ninety minutes of tummy time each day. Do tummy time when the child is alert and happy, not when he is not feeling well or is fussy. You will know that it is time to pick the baby up and end the activity when he gets fussy or starts crying. Do not do tummy time right after feeding, as the pressure on his stomach may cause him to spit up. If the infant falls asleep during tummy time, make sure to place him on his back to continue sleeping.

When a baby is ready for tummy time, you will already have prepared him for the activity. Each time you place the infant high up on your shoulder to burp, he is working the neck muscles to hold up his head. The higher up you hold him on your shoulder, the more he works the muscles required to keep his head up and steady.

Have you heard the saying "back to sleep and tummy to play"? Most pediatricians suggest that babies should sleep on their backs. Sleeping on the stomach increases the risk of sudden infant death syndrome, known as SIDS. The baby should sleep on a smooth, flat surface with no toys, pillows, or blankets close that might block his airway. Tummy play time is important because developing strong neck muscles allows the infant to move away from anything that might block his airway when sleeping.

Providing a Supportive Touch

As you initiate tummy time, you will notice that some activities involve the parent's or caregiver's touch:

- An introductory activity for tummy time is to place the infant with tummy down across your legs. You will need to support the baby's head and make sure the head is turned to the side. This is sometimes called *lap time.* Hold the baby's head parallel to the rest of her body. If the baby decides to go to sleep, turn her over on her back and put her to bed.

- Lie down on the floor and place the infant on your chest so you are face to face. Have fun making faces and talking with the baby. Hold both your hands firmly around her midsection.

Encouraging Physical Activity in Infants

- You can also do tummy time when carrying the baby. Carry the infant tummy down, placing one hand between the baby's legs and under her tummy so she can see where she is going. Your free hand should go under the baby's chest for additional support.

- Lay the baby tummy down on a large exercise ball. Slowly roll her forward and backward and then side to side. Hold the baby with both hands around her hips and lower back. Make sure you have a good grip, especially when you begin moving faster.

Interacting with Toys

Other tummy-time activities encourage movement by incorporating the baby's toys:

- Place the child's favorite colorful toy or rattle in front of him on the floor so he raises his head to look at the toy. The baby may also find it fun to see himself in the mirror. Place the infant on his tummy in front of a mirror so he can see his reflection.

- With the infant on his tummy on the floor, roll up a small blanket and place it under his chest and upper arms for additional support. Place a small toy in front for him to grab onto.

- Place a toy just out of the infant's reach to get him to stretch and reach for the toy.

- Place toys around the baby so he will have to turn his head and stretch the neck muscles to reach for a toy. This helps develop the muscles used to roll over and eventually crawl.

- As an infant gets older, tummy time becomes a time to learn how to roll. With the infant lying on his stomach with his head raised, place a toy in front of him and slowly move the toy to the side. As he follows the toy with his eyes, slightly tuck his opposite shoulder under him, which will encourage the baby to roll over on his back. The baby is not ready for this activity unless he has strong control of his head and neck muscles, which usually occurs at about three to four months. Also practice rolling from the back to the stomach. Both activities should be done mostly with an adult using a toy to encourage the baby to roll over but without adult physical involvement. This is something baby needs to discover on his own.

Tummy time will help the infant reach those important developmental milestones of rolling, sitting, crawling, and standing. Infants who do not get needed tummy time may have motor delays in the future. Tummy time is the best thing you can do for the infant to strengthen upper-back, neck, and stomach muscles.

More Ways to Move and Interact

Because babies tire of tummy time quickly until they gain strength, you will want to play with the baby on her back also. An interactive, strength-building movement involves laying the infant on her back on the floor, placing her hand around your forefinger, and holding her hand in place with your thumb and third finger. Stretch out the baby's arms by gently pulling her hands toward you. Repeat this activity four to five times with each arm, but do not pull the baby up off the floor. After about four months of age, the infant will have the strength to begin to pull herself up. In addition to stretching the arms forward, practice crossing the arms over the chest. Hold the infant's arms out to the sides, then bring them in across her chest, then spread them out again. Remember that these activities should be done slowly.

The bicycle exercise is another fun activity on the back. Hold the infant's feet and gently push one leg up toward her chest while extending the other. Push and extend, alternating each leg three to five times. Repeat several times during each play and movement session. You may find that the infant will begin to kick her legs freely in anticipation of this activity.

As you try new movements, you will find that the infant enjoys some more than others. Repetition is good because it builds strength, agility, and a sense of security, but adding variety to the routine will keep the baby interested and will foster learning new skills.

Developing
Strength
and
Balance

CHAPTER

5

A baby emerges into the world after having been cramped up in a small space for nine months. At birth, the baby's muscles are weak because they have not been used much. The more a baby uses her muscles, the stronger they will become. An infant will spend most of her first year of life strengthening muscles she will need to pick up objects, crawl, stand, and walk.

Muscle strength is also needed for balance, which is one of the first physical skills a child will begin to develop and is probably the most important. Balance gives the infant the ability to maintain stability, to sit without falling over, and to eventually stand on two feet and be able to walk.

Building Muscle Strength

Muscular strength is the ability to apply force and effort in order to move. Strong muscles are necessary for the infant to do all kinds of physical activities such as raising his head, crawling, standing, and walking, and eventually throwing, kicking, and climbing.

Strength is not a physical skill. However, for an infant to develop physical skills, he must develop the muscular strength to move his body and body parts. Practicing physical skills further strengthens muscles. Developing strength and developing physical skills go together—they depend on each other.

Every move the infant makes requires muscle strength, which increases as a muscle or group of muscles work together to lift, push, or pull. Strong muscles will help the baby reach developmental milestones of sitting up, crawling, standing, and walking. Strong muscles will also help the toddler and preschooler develop a foundation of physical skills.

Large muscles develop before small muscles. The muscles used to control the infant's neck, back, arms, and legs develop before the muscles in the fingers and hands. All infants learn how to do gross motor skills such as crawling and walking before they learn fine motor skills such as drawing or efficiently using a spoon.

Because newborns lack strength, parents and caregivers should always support an infant's head while holding and carrying him. Gently cradle the infant's head as you reach to pick him up.

MUSCLE STRENGTH— DID YOU KNOW?

When an infant moves and participates in activities that strengthen muscles, this helps him also improve balance, reduce falls, and improve sleep.

The process of strengthening muscles does not happen overnight. Strength building begins with infant reflexes stimulating the muscles to move. The baby learns from this stimulation that his brain can tell his muscles to move. Each time the infant turns his head from side to side, he is participating in an exercise that will help to develop muscle strength in his neck. At about six weeks, he will be strong enough to lift his head for a few seconds when he is placed on his stomach. By three months, the baby typically will have enough muscular strength to hold his head up on his own.

GENTLE TOUCH— DID YOU KNOW?

Safety first when it comes to developing a baby's muscles and strength. When lifting or pulling a baby's arms, adults should avoid jerky or twisting movements. An infant's muscles, bones, and ligaments are still developing and can slip out of place. Movements should be done slowly and smoothly. Do not pick a baby up by the arms or pull hard on his arms. Allow the child to do all the pulling and to bear his own weight.

Building a Sense of Balance

One of a baby's greatest accomplishments during the first year of life will be to stand upright and to walk. This achievement requires the infant to learn to balance. The baby develops her sense of balance in response to the pull of gravity. A good foundation of balance skills is important in moving through the environment, maintaining good posture, and doing all the movements needed to be physically active. Learning balance skills prepares an infant to sit up, crawl, stand, and walk.

The ability to balance is maintained by the vestibular system located in the inner ear, which also helps the child hear sounds. The system is complex, but basically the fluid located in the inner ear moves back and forth and sends signals telling the brain where the head is and if it is upright. The brain then sends signals to the child's eyes, muscles, joints, and bones so they can work together and make adjustments to keep the body balanced. The system helps the child remain steady and upright.

The vestibular system tells the infant when her head is upright or upside down, or tilted to one side or the other. Swinging, sliding, crawling up and down ramps or stairs, or crawling on uneven surfaces are all activities that will help to stimulate and exercise the vestibular system and improve

Encouraging Physical Activity in Infants

balance skills. Infants under four months of age can benefit simply from being frequently held and carried by their parents or caregivers—every time the adult moves, bends, or stops, the vestibular system works to send a signal to the infant's muscles to adjust her head and body to stay upright.

Although many children may struggle and experience some frustration in learning balance skills, balance disorders are considered uncommon in children. Providing lots of opportunities during the infant, toddler, and preschool years for a child to practice and experience being on and off balance will help provide a valuable foundation that will last throughout life.

Many adults find it difficult to watch an infant fall over when sitting, struggle while trying to roll over, or stumble to the ground when attempting to stand for the first time. Repetition of these movements helps the vestibular system process signals and form movement patterns and helps the child better coordinate her movements. Certainly, parents and caregivers should be available to keep their infants safe and provide protection from injury. However, the struggle during this process is very important for the infant.

This point is worth repeating—the baby's struggle to coordinate her movements and learn balance is critical. Parents and caregivers should not interfere with this struggle. Assist when needed, participate in activities

PRACTICE NEEDED

PRACTICE NEEDED

Why are baby walkers and jumpers not recommended for young children? Rather than helping the child learn to walk, baby walkers and jumpers reduce the time that infants spend on the floor rolling over, creeping, crawling, and pulling themselves up to sit and stand. All of these prewalking movements require balance—balance that a child may be slow to develop if she is sitting for long periods of time in a walker or jumper.

that place the baby in situations where she can practice balance, but allow the infant to learn these skills without your interference. A good example of interference with the process of an infant learning to balance can be seen in the use of walkers and jumpers. These items are considered inappropriate for infants because they restrict natural movement and may even delay development of a strong foundation of balance skills.

Balance is the foundation of every physical skill a child will develop. Every newborn has the natural instinct to move and struggle to place her body in an upright position. She will need balance skills to succeed in almost every sport or physical activity she will participate in throughout life, such as climbing, throwing a ball, walking across a beam, and riding a bike. Infants will have an easier time developing balance skills when they have strong back, neck, and stomach muscles. So to help the infant develop those balance skills, help her strengthen her muscles.

There are two types of balance skills—*static balance* and *dynamic balance*. Dynamic balance is the ability to maintain balance and control of one's body

while moving. The infant will start to develop her dynamic-balance skills when she begins to crawl, stand, and then walk. All infants work to initially control their muscles—especially their heads—so they can become upright. Static balance is the ability to hold a position and maintain control while not moving. When the infant sits unassisted for the first time, this is an example of static balance.

When working with an infant, the best way to help develop balance skills is to place her in an off-balance position and allow her to use her muscles to move back on balance. As you watch a child learn this skill, the first thing you might notice is that an infant must have her center of gravity over the base of support to balance. When the baby gets on all fours—on her hands and knees—she will have a wide base of support and will be balanced and not fall over. If she reaches for a toy with one hand, she changes her base of support and may topple over. It is much easier for the infant to remain on balance when balancing on two hands and two knees than when balancing on two knees and only one hand.

Reflex actions help stimulate an infant's muscles to begin the process of developing static-balance skills. After that, she learns to balance by repeating activities over and over again. Movements such as swinging, spinning, and rocking will help the child develop a sense of dynamic balance. During her first year, an infant will begin to scoot across

SWINGING ACTIVITIES

The purpose of swinging and rocking activities is to help the infant develop a sense of balance. With a newborn baby, you can hold her against your chest while gently rocking her back and forth. As infants mature, swinging activities can increase in duration and speed. Slow and easy does it. Gently swinging, rocking, and placing baby off balance and then guiding her back on balance will help lay a foundation to improve confidence and develop balance skills. Whenever you swing the infant remember the following:

● Move at varying speeds; start slowly and increase speed based on the infant's age and enjoyment of the activity.

● Move in a variety of directions—up, down, and sideways.

● Gently swing without jerky movements. It will be at least ten years before the child is ready for a roller-coaster ride.

the room, crawl, and roll. She will rock back and forth in your arms, and will bounce up and down on your knees. At this stage of development, infants love to do activities over and over again. Parents and caregivers should encourage this repetition.

Activities
for Increasing
Strength
and Balance

During the first year of life, all physical activities typically involve both increasing strength and developing balance. Parents and caregivers can support their infant's physical development by participating in the activities suggested in the following sections. These are just a few of the many types of strength and balance activities that are fun, safe, and age appropriate for the infant. Remember that infants learn motor skills through repetition, so do not be afraid to do the same activities daily.

Birth to Four Months

Overhead Play Gyms

It may be helpful to provide the growing infant with an overhead play gym to use during floor activity time. Play gyms encourage lots of stretching and reaching—activities babies need to strengthen muscles. Reaching helps to develop muscles in the back and shoulders and helps the baby to cross the midline, reaching with one hand for a hanging object on the other side of the body.

Bicycle Kicks

Adults will notice that at about two to three months of age infants will begin kicking their feet when lying on their backs. Take advantage of this natural movement to strengthen the legs by gently moving the infant's feet back and forth as if he is riding a bicycle. After a few weeks of practice, any time you lay the infant on his back he will begin pedaling.

Turning and Swinging

It is important to balance development to place the infant in different positions as you carry him. Hold the baby against your right shoulder and

Encouraging Physical Activity in Infants

then against your left as you move him from place to place. Bend forward and then from side to side as you move. This will place the baby in an off-balance position and require him to tighten his muscles to regain his balance.

Hold the baby out in front of you, facing up, with one arm under his shoulders and the other hand supporting his bottom. Then turn him over so you support him with a hand under his chest and the other through his legs so you can support his stomach. Also hold him so he is on his side as you move. This changing of positions helps the infant develop balance.

Rock the Ball

This activity helps with both balance and strength. Underinflate a large beach ball or exercise ball. A slightly underinflated ball will help you better hold on to the baby during initial ball activities. At about four months, the infant will be ready to do ball activities on a fully inflated beach ball.

Place the infant on his back on the ball, holding him with both your hands around the middle.

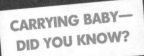

CARRYING BABY— DID YOU KNOW?

In some cultures, parents carry their infants in slings held against their bodies as they go through their day. This permits parents to move from place to place and continue to work while keeping an eye on their child. Every time the parent moves, the infant is using muscles to keep from falling and thus is developing balance skills.

Gently and slowly at first, rock back and forth, from side to side, and round and round. Start with slow and steady movements, rocking for two to three minutes at first but increasing the time as the baby gets older. Rock so he is sometimes upside down. After he has finished rocking on his back, turn him over on his stomach. It is important to sometimes rock slowly and sometimes move faster, allowing the child to lose his balance. When the infant begins to feel he is off balance, his muscles tighten and he moves to be on balance.

By the third or fourth month, a baby typically can hold his head up and is beginning to sit up by himself. Sit the baby on the beach ball, and make sure to hold on with both your hands around his waist. If the infant is not yet sitting, you may need to support him with your hands around his upper body. Rock the baby back and forth and from one side to the other. You will be able to feel his muscles work to keep upright and stay on balance. This can also be a good time to gently bounce the infant up and down on the ball.

When the child is four months old, you can inflate the ball more fully. By this age, you should be able to change where you hold the child while he is on the ball. Provide the infant with less support as you rock him back and forth. Switch from holding around the midsection to only holding onto the arms or legs. Rock the infant back and forth on both the stomach and back. You will notice more movement from the child to right himself, especially when his head is below the rest of his body. If the baby appears frightened, go back to holding him around the waist.

Arm Pull and Pull-Up

Lay the baby on his back and place your index fingers in the baby's hands. This will stimulate the grasp reflex, and

he will grasp your fingers. Gently pull up so the muscles are stretched without lifting the baby off his back, then gently pull your fingers out of the grasp and watch as the infant pulls his arms back toward his body. This is an activity you can practice before or after tummy time or any time you have a diaper change. Setting a goal of two to three times per session, several times each day is a good target as you work with the baby to develop his arm and shoulder muscles. You can also provide an infant with his favorite rattle to grasp.

Four Months to Eight Months

As the baby grows and continues to develop balance and strength, you can introduce new physical activities. Continue to repeat activities introduced earlier until she decides the activities are not fun anymore. The child will let you know when it is time to move on to new and different fun activities.

Bouncing Baby

Bouncing may seem like an unsafe activity for a four-month-old baby. And, if you are thinking about bouncing on a trampoline you would be correct. Baby bouncing involves gently rocking her back and forth and moving her up and down slowly. When the infant has developed her muscles and balance to the point where she can sit unassisted, baby-bounce activities would be appropriate. Sit the infant on your lap facing you, and hold both your hands around her chest and under her arms. Gently sway the baby back and forth from side to side and forward and backward. At first sway gently back and forth and move the infant only a couple of inches in each direction. Then gently lift her a couple of inches off your lap to give her the sensation of moving up and down. This is a great time to sing and talk with the baby. Having your hands around the infant's body will let her feel and anticipate your movements and begin to understand in which direction she is about to move.

Baby Sit-Ups on a Ball

Continue to use the exercise ball or beach ball introduced in the earlier section, and by the time the child is about four months old, you can use a more inflated ball. After going through your regular routine of rocking the baby on both her back and stomach, forward, backward, sideways, and round and round, try a baby sit-up. Lay the infant on her back on the ball with your hands on her legs. Gently push down on her thighs and roll the ball toward you; this movement will help her begin to sit up. Gently push on the child's legs again and roll the ball slightly away from you to lower her back to the starting position. Three or four baby sit-ups each day will help improve balance and strengthen the stomach muscles.

Baby in the Mirror

Add to the excitement of being on the beach or exercise ball by doing the ball activities in front of a mirror. With the infant on her back on the ball, grasp her feet and roll her backward. In that position, she will be able to look at herself upside down in the mirror. Turn her over on her stomach and roll back and forth. The baby will lift her head higher and thus work the neck and back muscles just to look at herself in the mirror. By the time a baby is seven to eight months old, she will be familiar with the ball activities and will want to participate for longer time periods. A three-to-five-minute session is considered a good workout at this age.

By eight months, the child will be ready for a more challenging type of balance activity with the ball. Instead of holding the infant by the feet or hands, place her on her back and grasp the right arm and the right leg. Rock back and forth slowly at first and then get a bit faster, but not too fast. By holding on in a different way and adding a little more speed, you are changing up the activity. As always, if the child shows any signs of not being happy, slow the activity down or stop it and consider trying it at another time.

Pull Up, Push Down

The baby is ready to really begin working on those back and stomach muscles. However, be careful not to have her sit for long periods of time, as back muscles may not yet be strong enough to hold her weight. In this activity, get down on the floor with the infant and sit with your legs straight out in front. Place the baby on the floor on her back, facing you, and positioned between your legs. Offer your thumbs for her to grasp. As she grasps your

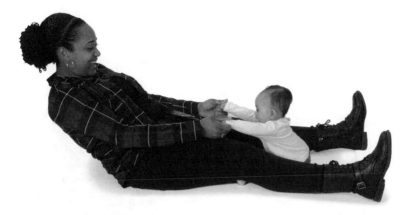

thumbs, place the rest of your fingers around her forearms and gently pull her up to a seated position. She will tuck her head forward as she sits up. Then gently push her back down, using your legs as a cushion for the back of her head. Many children will attempt to stand if you continue to gently pull on the way up.

Happy Swinging Baby

Infants, of course, are too young to be able to sit in a swing on a playground and swing alone. When they become preschoolers, they will learn how to use their arms, chests, and legs to make a swing move. Even though infants are not ready to coordinate their muscles and pump their legs to swing, sitting in an appropriate infant swing and swinging gently forward and backward is still a great infant balance activity. Infants should not swing in a swing made for older children. The swing should be made specifically for infants and have a belt or harness to hold the baby in. Also, infants should not be placed into a swing until they are able to sit up without help from an adult (sometime around about six to eight months). At first place the baby in the swing and let her sit without swinging. When you see that she feels comfortable sitting in the swing, gently push so the swing moves a couple of inches. Swinging helps the infant further develop the vestibular system and improve balance. Infants should never be pushed to travel a distance more than two to three feet forward and back. This is an activity that is fun for adult and baby but must be supervised at all times.

Weight on Hands

Place the baby facedown on her tummy. Grasp her from behind with your hands secured around her hips. Lift her hips in the air about 8 to 10 inches, and she will extend her arms forward to hold herself up on her hands. Don't lift too high, as the infant needs to be able to put some of her weight on her hands. At first the child may only want to balance on her elbows, but she will soon extend her hands to take weight on her arms. Allow the baby to hold herself up for six to ten seconds before you lower her back to the floor.

Rocking with Mom and Dad

You may think this activity will provide more exercise for parents and caregivers than it will for the infant. Although this may be the case, the benefits to the infant's balance will outweigh the extra effort you expend. Lie on your back with your knees bent and feet flat on the floor. Place the infant on your stomach sitting with her back against your legs and facing you. Holding her hands or arms and keeping your knees bent, begin rocking back and forth toward your knees and away, just like you are doing a sit-up. The infant will soon hold onto your fingers and help you push back and forth. Repeat this activity daily for as long as you and baby are having fun. Add some background sounds and rock to the infant's favorite music.

Encouraging Physical Activity in Infants

Tummy Surfing

With all the rocking and rolling you and the child have been doing lately, it might also be time for some surfing. This activity will help the infant strengthen the lower back muscles. Sit on the floor with your knees bent, and stand the baby facing you so she is leaning forward on your legs with her head looking over your knees. Holding the baby's hands, lean back until your back is on the floor and the baby is surfing on your

legs. Bend the knees and gently bounce the baby up and down. Hold her arms out to the side. After several weeks, the baby may feel comfortable enough so you can begin rocking back and forth with her on this high perch.

It will be a couple of months before the infant is ready for tummy gliding. Start by sitting on the floor as you did in the tummy-surfing activity. Hold the infant's hands, and place your feet on her hips. Roll back and pull and lift the baby into the air with your feet. Bend and straighten your legs to lift her up and down. This helps her to strengthen her back and leg muscles but also helps improve balance.

Kicking Sideways

By the end of the eighth month, most infants will be pulling up to stand and holding onto the sofa or a short table. As the infant is holding onto the furniture, place a small foam or rubber ball on the floor next to her feet. She may accidently kick the ball at first, but when you keep putting it back by her feet she will start to get the idea of raising one foot to kick the ball on purpose. Make sure that you place the ball on both sides of the body so she can kick with the right foot and the left. Some adults tie a string to the ball so they can hold it to the child's side and not have to chase the ball.

Eight Months to One Year

By the time the infant is eight to twelve months old, he is sitting and possibly crawling and attempting to crawl upstairs. He will pull himself up to a standing position and experiment with letting go to stand alone. These efforts will very soon lead to taking his first steps. This is the age where the infant will begin to imitate adults. If you place a block in a container, he will want to do the same. Playing with a child at this age will go a long way in instilling the attitude and behaviors related to daily physical activity. Make sure you set aside several times during the day to

Encouraging Physical Activity in Infants

participate in fun physical activities with the infant. The child will also begin learning about movement by watching other infants. The eight-to-twelve-month age range is the time you want to join other parents and infants in informal playgroups.

Baby Sit-Ups

Baby sit-ups are fun! Baby sit-ups should not be confused with sit-up exercises adults do during fitness workouts. Baby sit-ups help the infant increase back and leg flexibility and strength. Sit on the floor facing the infant and place your legs over his legs, which should be spread apart. Hold the infant's hands or offer your fingers to grasp. Gently push backward so the infant lowers himself back toward the floor, and then pull gently as the child returns to a sitting position. Some babies may feel uncomfortable at first with lowering themselves backward, but in a couple of weeks they will get the hang of the activity.

Time to Chase

As soon as an infant begins to crawl, he will be delighted to play chase with you. Get down on your hands and knees on the floor. As he starts to crawl away, grab his legs and pull him back to you. When he crawls away again, catch him and pull him back again. What a fun way to end an activity session and get ready for a well-deserved nap!

From Sitting to Standing

Balance and strength are equally important to the infant in reaching the milestone of standing without assistance from an adult. This activity will help the child begin to take weight on his feet while strengthening hismuscles and improving balance. At about ten months of age, or when the infant is sitting without assistance, have him sit on a baby-sized stool so his back has no support (he is sitting without help from an adult). His feet should be touching the floor so they are able to push against it. His knees and hips should be at

90-degree angles. When the child is in this position, ask him to reach over and pick up a toy on the floor (experiment with placement of the toy in front and to both sides to increase reach and strengthen muscles) and then sit back on the stool. This movement requires the baby to move his feet apart for stability and place his weight over his feet, strengthening the legs as well as the back and shoulder muscles. This activity will help prepare the infant to position his feet directly under his body to take his weight for standing and eventually walking.

It Is Time to Walk

A child is not going to stand up and walk until he is physically ready to do so. All the balance and strength activities you have practiced with him over the last several months will certainly help him, because lack of balance and muscular strength slows the process of walking. This activity can help prepare a child for walking weeks before he actually takes his first steps. Stand behind the child, place your hands around his upper arms, and pull him up so he is standing. Gently pull one arm forward and then the other; his feet will follow as he rotates his hips to step. Keep this activity going until the infant is ready to stop. You can repeat it several times a day.

Cruising

An infant can also practice walking by cruising back and forth alongside the furniture. Stand the infant next to the sofa or a short table or bench. Let him hold on with one hand as you hold his other hand for balance. Slowly move back and forth along the furniture and practice walking. Soon the infant will let go of your hand to practice the activity on his own. You can place a favorite toy on one end of the sofa as an incentive for him to walk forward.

Encouraging Physical Activity in Infants

Boxes—Baby's First Obstacle Course

During the first year (after crawling begins), in addition to learning about balance and developing strength, infants are focused on learning about their environment and how they can move in the space around them. The infant will not yet understand the concept of directions; pathways; levels; shapes; and moving over, under, around, and through obstacles. However, he will move using all these concepts. Babies love boxes, which can provide hours of fun and learning. In your play space, provide a number of sturdy cardboard boxes along with the colorful toys you have purchased for the infant.

- Place a toy on the other side of a box, and encourage him to crawl around the box to get the toy.
- Cut both ends out of a box to form a tunnel, and watch the delight as the infant crawls through the passageway.
- Place the baby sitting down in a box, and position his favorite toy in view outside the box. Encourage the baby to climb out of the box to get the toy.
- Place a toy in the box, and ask the baby to get the toy.
- Find a box that is three or four times bigger than the infant, so there is plenty of room inside. Cut some holes in the top of the box to let in light. Use the box to play peekaboo with the infant, placing it over his body and then asking where he is. He will still be able to see you through the holes. If this is uncomfortable for the infant, stop the activity and save it for weeks later.

Vision Development
and Coordination
of Movement

CHAPTER

7

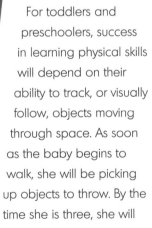

For toddlers and preschoolers, success in learning physical skills will depend on their ability to track, or visually follow, objects moving through space. As soon as the baby begins to walk, she will be picking up objects to throw. By the time she is three, she will be on her way to learning to catch, kick, and strike a ball. Not only will good tracking skills help children learn ball skills, but they are critical to learning how to read.

The oculomotor system lets infants direct the movements of their eyes. During a baby's first two years, she will learn to maintain a steady visual contact with an object. You may notice the baby fixating on a particular object or staring at your face when you come close to cuddle. The infant will also learn to quickly and accurately make eye jumps from one object to another—first looking at an adult's face, then away to a colorful object, then back to the adult's face again. Eventually a baby will use her eyes to pursue an object and smoothly follow a moving target. She may follow you with her eyes as you move across the room or focus on a ball rolling across the floor. All of these skills will help children later when they are learning to catch, kick, and strike a ball.

Of all the systems of the body, the visual system is the least mature at birth. Certainly a baby's sense of hearing is much more mature than her sense of sight. It will take several months for an infant to learn how to use this complex system, and good vision skills do not just happen. An infant will need a lot of experiences playing with and watching objects that move toward her and away from her. To be successful, she will have to focus her eyes on objects as they move. Tracking objects also helps the infant learn that the shape, size, and color of objects do not change even when the angle of the view and the distance have changed. These skills will also eventually help the child be able to read a line across a page.

When a baby first looks up at you, the nerve cells in her retina and brain that control vision are still underdeveloped, and she does not see much detail. For the first several weeks, infants can see only sharply contrasting

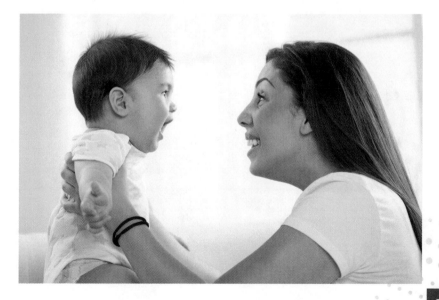

TRACKING RANGE—DID YOU KNOW?

Babies younger than two months are able to visually track an object in front of them for about 90 degrees over short periods if the object is moving very slowly. By three months, infants are usually able to track an object for about 180 degrees, all without moving their heads.

patterns of light and darkness—black and white and shades of gray. During this time, a baby will not have the ability to focus her eyes on objects, so do not be concerned if she does not look directly at you.

In the first few weeks, an infant will focus best on objects that are 8 to 12 inches away. This is about the distance between your face and a baby when you feed her. Lay the baby on her back and get close to talk and smile. This will help her begin to focus her vision.

Progression of Vision Development

By the time infants are about six to eight months of age, they usually have developed 20/20 eyesight. By the end of the first year, they are able to accurately judge distance and are increasingly improving their eye-hand coordination. Fine motor skills have improved so that an infant can manipulate small objects (such as grasping and shaking a rattle) and can begin to feed himself. When an infant begins to walk, he will use his eyes to help direct whole-body movements such as climbing, jumping, kicking, and throwing.

The following sections can help caregivers and parents understand the progression infants go through in terms of vision development. You will also find some vision activities to stimulate development along the way.

Vision problems are not common in infants. But if you do have a concern about an infant's vision, a pediatrician or optometrist should check it out. Problems can be more easily corrected if found early. Doctors recommend that infants get their first eye exam at about six months. Some optometrists will provide this service for free, but you will need to check to find one who offers this free exam. Pediatricians also usually check the baby's eyes.

Birth to Four Months

When a baby is born, his vision will be blurred, and he will be able to focus only on objects that are 8 to 12 inches away. He will not recognize colors, only black and white and shades of gray. At first a baby will gaze at an object for only a few seconds; however, by about ten weeks of age, children can follow moving objects with their eyes. Also, newborns usually will not be able to move their eyes without moving their heads until somewhere between ten and sixteen weeks.

A baby's ability to use his eyes together is called *eye teaming,* and it will take up to four months or longer for the infant to coordinate his eyes so they work together as a team. Do not be alarmed if a child's eyes sometimes go in different directions. He simply has not yet developed the muscular control to keep his eyes from crossing. This is a normal part of the process, but if a child still crosses his eyes at six months, check with his pediatrician.

Tracking skills begin to develop when the infant starts to visually follow objects, usually about three months of age. Fine-motor coordination, along with recognition of the full range of colors, begins shortly after this at about four months, when the infant will begin reaching for objects and may begin to show preference for one color over another. This is the time to provide a mobile above the infant to help him coordinate his eye movements. He will begin reaching for the mobile as it moves. Also hold brightly colored toys in front of the child so he must reach out to grab a toy.

You can support the infant's visual development between birth and four months in the following ways:

- Always talk to the baby when you walk around. Babies react to the sound and turn their heads to focus on the sound and movement. This turning of the head also helps to strengthen neck muscles.

- Frequently change the position of the infant's crib and change the direction you lay the infant in the crib. This allows him to look out in different directions and focus on different objects around the crib.

- Hang a mobile above the child's crib so he can watch the movement and focus on the objects moving through space. The mobile should be high enough that he cannot grab the objects; it is for practice

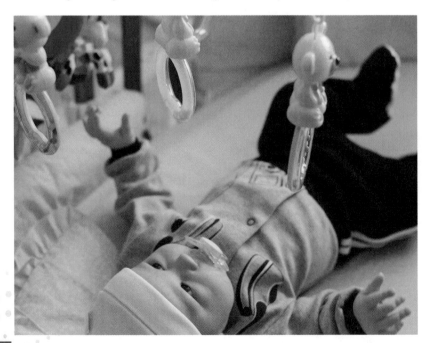

focusing and getting his eyes to work as a team. Before the baby is four months of age, the mobile should consist of black and white colors so the infant can focus on the contrast. After about four months, provide a mobile with a variety of colors.

- Each time you feed the baby, alternate left and right sides. This will give him a different perspective and make sure both eyes receive stimulation.

- Provide a dim light in the baby's room at night. The light will not keep him awake, but when he is awake, it will help him see contrast between dark shades and the light.

- Make sure you have colorful toys that the baby can easily grasp and hold up to his face. Before he is ready to grasp, parents and caregivers should hold the toys in front of him about 12 inches from his face. Slowly move the toys so the infant can begin tracking objects.

Four to Eight Months

By the end of the sixth month, most babies are using both eyes in unison and their vision is 20/20. They are able to focus on things that are close as well as things that are farther away. They are also beginning to understand depth perception, so they have a better sense of how far they have to reach to grasp a toy and have better accuracy. A child this age will soon start to remember what he sees and may be observed searching and grabbing for his favorite toy.

Muscles needed to move are getting stronger, and the infant will soon begin to push up with his arms and move his head around to better see and explore his new world. He will also roll over, scoot across the floor, and sit unassisted. He will begin to coordinate his vision with his movement. You will see jumps in learning almost daily as the infant begins to use his hands to reach for everything he sees.

VISION AND CRAWLING— DID YOU KNOW?

All parents and caregivers want to see a baby take his first step, but don't be in too much of a hurry. Child development experts suggest that infants who do a lot of crawling may be more likely to have teamed their eyes when looking at close objects. The American Optometric Association notes that babies who crawl frequently will get more practice with coordination of vision than early walkers, who may not learn to use their eyes together as well.

Most infants will begin to crawl during this time. Crawling opens a new world for vision development. Scooting or crawling across a room helps an infant learn to judge distances when he sees something he likes and crawls forward to get it. The baby will soon learn about his own body in relation to other objects, as well as about the size and shape of objects.

You can support an infant's visual development during this time in several ways. His eyesight is now pretty good, and he is ready for you to provide items in the crib for him to grab, pull, and kick. The baby is also ready for lots of daily tummy time. Make sure to provide several colorful toys (such as plastic or wooden blocks that are small enough to fit in an infant's hands but not small enough to be choking hazards) on the floor for him to grasp, look at, and shake. Also set out colorful items that are out of his grasp so he must raise his head to focus on items that are farther away. Remember that tummy time is also for caregivers and parents, so get on the floor and play with the baby.

At this age, infants will start to develop an understanding of how to let go of objects. You will see them beginning to move toys from one hand to the other. When they have objects in both hands, they may begin banging the items together and listening to the sounds being made. Your baby's eyes will be focused on these processes.

Make sure to practice tracking skills daily at this age. Hold a favorite toy in front of the child, and slowly move it to the right and left, and up and down in front of him. This is also a good time to begin playing hand-clapping games, such as patty-cake. Sing or say the words out loud, moving the baby's hands through the motion as you play. This movement helps the child's vision and fine motor control as he coordinates looking at his hands and touching them together.

Eight Months to One Year

During this time period, the infant's world explodes with movement. By twelve months of age, most babies will be crawling and trying to walk. Parents and caregivers should encourage crawling rather than early walking to help the child develop better eye-hand coordination. Once an infant begins to walk, he will use his eyes to coordinate the movement of his body. This coordination will allow him to be more accurate with grasping and throwing.

Also, an infant will have a great time picking up objects (such as blocks) and putting them in a basket—then dumping them out and starting all over again. Both his fine motor skills and his eye-hand-body coordination are maturing rapidly. He will soon begin climbing, which will require him to judge distance as he reaches for the next rung on the ladder. The maturity of his vision skills now allows him to manipulate smaller objects. He also will begin to pull himself up to a standing position and will be able to coordinate his eyes and hands to grasp objects with the thumb and forefinger. Most infants this age will begin feeding themselves with finger foods.

Safety should be a major concern because smaller objects could become a risk for choking. This is the time to increase adult supervision, as a baby now has the vision and the still-immature but quickly developing motor skills to mostly go wherever he wants. Supervision is mandatory whenever the infant is crawling to prevent minor bumps and bruises and more serious injuries. Be sure there are no sharp corners for the baby to fall on or sharp objects that could cause an eye injury. He is curious about everything and does not yet know what can hurt him. Make sure to lock up all cabinets and drawers that contain cleaning supplies and to block any stairways you do not want the child to climb.

You can support the infant's visual development between eight and twelve months by doing the following:

- Encourage lots of crawling and creeping, as this will help a child to better judge distance. Get on the floor with the infant. This will encourage him to crawl to you. Place toys farther and farther out of reach to challenge him to crawl more. Be careful not to frustrate the child; physical activity and movement at this age are all about little successes.

- Provide toys that can be taken apart and put together to assist with vision development.

- Blow bubbles so the infant can track them as they move. You will see him reach out to touch the bubbles and maybe even observe him using his index finger to poke and pop the bubbles.
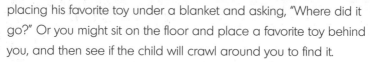
- Play hide-and-seek games, such as placing his favorite toy under a blanket and asking, "Where did it go?" Or you might sit on the floor and place a favorite toy behind you, and then see if the child will crawl around you to find it.
- Provide toys that let infants explore cause and effect. For instance, supply rattles that the baby can shake or toys that the child can spin.

At this age, new activities are possible because infants are developing new capabilities. Hide-and-seek games are appealing because visual memory is beginning to develop. Infants also begin to understand cause and effect—the reason something happens and what happens—and vision is important to this process. Learning cause and effect will be a fun experience for the infant as he discovers that dumping something over makes a sound or gets a reaction from an adult.

During a baby's first year, he will learn how to use visual information to see and move in his new world. The infant's ability to coordinate his vision with his movement will guide his physical skill development for many years to come. The most important of the vision skills is the ability to track with the eyes to follow, reach, and grasp objects. Tracking activities help an infant develop depth perception and eye-hand coordination and are critical to the evolution of catching and striking skills. As the infant becomes a toddler and then a preschooler, he will be better prepared to meet the challenges of learning those two skills if he has had lots of early practice at tracking moving objects.

Fine Motor Skills

Fine motor skills are those used to manipulate objects with the hands and fingers, and they develop along with tracking skills. They require eye-hand coordination to be successful. Not much development of these skills goes on during the first months of life as the infant spends most of her time with her hands clenched in fists.

At about three months, she will begin to open her hands and experiment with lifting objects to her mouth. By four months, the infant has developed the muscle coordination to grip small objects and reach for and grasp small toys. Combine these skills with improved vision, and the infant is off to a great start developing fine motor skills.

By six months, you will observe infants exploring everything with their hands, so provide toys with different shapes and textures. By eight months, the infant has more strength to open and close her hands and now delights in dropping her toys. And by twelve months, she begins to develop more control of her fingers and will use her thumb and forefinger to grasp objects instead of using her entire hand.

Encouraging Physical Activity in Infants

When these things begin to happen, get ready for lots of fun! The baby will want to use her new fine motor skills to feed herself, and when she loses interest in feeding, she will certainly discover that picking things up and throwing them will get lots of fun reactions from adults. These fine motor skills also allow the infant to hold a bottle or cup, which increases her independence.

The best way to encourage fine motor skills during the first year of life is to practice tracking skills and use a variety of toys of different colors, shapes, and textures. Activities include reaching for and grasping bubbles, playing with rattles and blocks, squeezing water out of a sponge, stacking blocks, sorting shapes, and tearing paper. Provide lots of opportunities for the infant to play with her fingers.

Caregivers need to play, too! Hold a toy about 3 inches away from the baby, and move it to get her attention so she will grab it. As the infant gets older, create activities that require her to transfer objects from one

hand to another, and make sure both hands are used. Use mobiles and infant gyms to provide objects for her to reach for and grab while lying on her back.

Providing fine motor activities when a child is an infant will encourage skills that will later help her with eating, holding a pencil or crayon, and being able to dress herself. Finger dexterity is needed for pulling zippers up and down, buttoning buttons, and eventually tying shoes.

Encouraging Physical Activity in Infants

Moving Forward

CHAPTER

8

Wow! What an exciting year. And what a fun time you and the baby have had participating in daily physical activity. The infant has grown in strength and balance and has improved tracking and vision skills, and you have provided him with a foundation of these important abilities, which will become the basis for new physical skills that the toddler is now ready to begin learning.

New adventures lie ahead for you and the child. Daily physical activity will continue to be important to the ongoing advancement of not only the child's motor skills but also his emotional, social, and cognitive development. During the next four years, locomotor, balance, and manipulative skills will be the focus for continued physical development, and the young child will learn how to run, gallop, hop, and skip. Practicing climbing, jumping, and balance skills will become favorite daily activities.

And the manipulation of balls to throw, catch, kick, and strike will provide hours and hours of endlessly fun challenges.

Continue to schedule and provide daily adult-supervised play time for practice of essential physical skills. Seek developmentally appropriate activities and equipment for the toddler and preschooler. Don't be drawn into using adult-size equipment (such as a wooden bat, or an official-size basketball or soccer ball) for skill practice. Find child-size equipment to enhance the success the child can have in the development of physical skills.

Get ready to hear a request (or demand) that you hold his hand so he can walk across the beam or help him climb on the playground equipment. You also will frequently hear, "Can we go outside and play now?"

Encouraging Physical Activity in Infants

By exploring what the body can do and practicing skills daily, the infant has reached a gateway leading to all future learning as a toddler. In terms of developing physical skills, the toddler needs adult help more than ever before. You are and will continue to be a child's best teacher.

If it has not already happened, the toddler will soon become a social creature and, in addition to playing with parents and caregivers, will seek other children. Toddlers learn best not only by doing but also by observing and getting ideas from other children. Find a playgroup so the child can share with and learn from peers. If the toddler will be spending time in a child care setting, investigate and make sure physical-skill development activities are in the curriculum and scheduled each day.

Get ready for a fast-moving, fun, activity-filled time over the next several years. Continue to emphasize the importance of an active lifestyle and physical-skill development by being a role model and participating in physical activities with the child every day. The little toddler-to-be is well on the way to becoming physically active and healthy throughout life.

References and Resources

Active for Life. 2014. "How to Give Your Baby an Active Start." http://
activeforlife.com/give-baby-active-start/

American Academy of Pediatrics. 2001. "Injuries Associated with Infant
Walkers." *Pediatrics* 108(3): 790–92.

American Optometric Association (AOA). 2014. "Infant Vision: Birth to 24
Months of Age." St. Louis, MO: AOA. http://www.aoa.org/patients-and-
public/good-vision-throughout-life/childrens-vision/infant-vision-birth-to-
24-months-of-age?sso=y

Gabbard, Carl, and Luis Rodrigues. 2015. "Optimizing Early Brain and
Motor Development Through Movement." *Early Childhood News,*
accessed April 14, 2015. http://www.earlychildhoodnews.com/
earlychildhood/article_view.aspx?ArticleID=360

KidsHealth. 2015. "Kids and Exercise." *KidsHealth.org,* accessed April 14,
2015. http://kidshealth.org/parent/nutrition_center/staying_fit/exercise.
html

National Association for the Education of Young Children. 2015. "Infant
Program Health and Safety Checklist." *NAEYC,* accessed April 23,
2015. http://families.naeyc.org/accredited-article/infant-program-
health-and-safety-checklist

National Association for Sport and Physical Education. 2011. *Active Start:
A Statement of Physical Activity Guidelines for Children from Birth to Age
5.* 2nd ed. Washington, DC: NASPE.

Slining, Meghan, et al. 2010. "Infant Overweight Is Associated with
Delayed Motor Development." *Journal of Pediatrics* 157(1): 20–25.

Encouraging Physical Activity in Infants

Index